THE WORLD WAR ONE SERIES No.1

AFTER THE BALL IS OVER

A One Act Play

GW00632608

Lynn Brittney

Published by Playstage
United Kingdom.

An imprint of Write Publications Ltd

www.playsforadults.com

Designed by Kate Lowe, Greensands Graphics
Printed by Creeds Ltd, Bridport, Dorset

Note to producers about staging "After The Ball is Over."

The first half of the play is relentlessly light and upper class – a society viewing war as an upcoming "lark."

The actors

TOM is basically a quiet country gentleman lawyer. A tragic widower who lost his wife ten years before and who whiles away his time undertaking legal work for the local people and playing cards with SIR EDWIN, whose estate affairs he manages.

SIR EDWIN and LADY MARJORIE are country gentry from the Victorian era, although they are not hidebound or stuffy, just a little quaint but certainly kind.

VICTORIA is an independent unmarried woman with her own inherited money. One suspects that she is unmarried because she is so fiercely intelligent but she is not strident or radical. She is basically a kind soul, who is involved in charity work and has doubts about the pending war.

Once the action shifts to TOM writing a letter from the trenches, the atmosphere of the play changes to one of the harshness of war. While he writes his letter, we can hear shelling in the distance and he writes, matter-of-factly about the unpleasant experiences that are wearing him down.

The costumes

When staging this play, one should consider the possibility of suggesting the change in everyone's outlook through the costumes. In the first half, the ballgowns can be brilliant, colourful and showy. In the second half, LADY M should certainly be in black or dark purple, as she is mourning the loss of her son-in-law. The other ladies could be in similarly drab gowns – implying that the life and colour has gone out of society in general.

TOM stays in khaki uniform throughout. SIR EDWIN stays in evening dress (tails) throughout. JACK may be in the "Mess Dress" of a cavalry captain in the first half and in evening dress for the second, since he has been discharged from the Army for longer than TOM.

Scenery

(See set plan). This scenery should be well within the scope of most amateur groups. If, however, you were considering pre-formed items, such as balustrades, benches, urns etc. that are lightweight and can be painted, we recommend that you look at this site : www.peterevansstudios.co.uk.

Music and Special Effects

Music of the period can be easily obtained on CD. Because the orchestra would be a small affair, we would recommend any of the recordings of The Palm Court Orchestra such as :Viennese Delights; The Picnic Party; Music for Tea Dancing; Salon Musik; or any Strauss Waltzes played by small ensembles. These can be obtained in CD format or MP3 downloads from Amazon. Obviously, a track of the piece of music called "After the Ball is Over" is necessary for the plot.

It is important that the music pieces come to a natural end, followed by applause, rather than being faded out or cut off in mid flow. So technical crew may need to time the actor's dialogue in order to play the appropriate amount of music.

Note that the applause should be of a smallish group of about fifty people not the sound effect of a large auditorium applauding. It should also be genteel applause and not include any whistling or calling out.

Sounds of shelling for the trenches scene can be found on several internet websites and on sound effects CDs available in most drama/music libraries.

THE WORLD WAR ONE SERIES. No.1: AFTER THE BALL IS OVER

CAST *(In order of appearance)*

TOM PRITCHARD	a country lawyer, now enlisted in the Army, aged 50+.
SIR EDWIN	jovial country squire, aged 70+
LADY MARJORIE	Sir Edwin's wife, kind, given to charitable works, aged 70+
VICTORIA PELHAM	intelligent, unmarried, inherited wealth, aged 45+
JACK	Sir Edwin's grandson, bit of a handful, son of an Earl, aged early 20s.
MAUD	pretty, upper class, a bit dim, aged early 20s.

3 male and 3 female parts.

The action mostly takes place on the terrace of SIR EDWIN's country house apart from one scene (in a spotlight) which is set in TOM's dugout at the front line.

WORLD WAR 1. No. 1.

AFTER THE BALL IS OVER

As the lights go up, TOM is standing on one side of the terrace, looking thoughtfully out over the gardens. It is still light and a beautiful summer evening – about 9 o'clock. He is dressed in the khaki uniform of a captain in the army. We hear music from the open French windows. The orchestra is playing a Strauss waltz. SIR EDWIN enters on to the terrace, carrying two glasses of scotch.

SIR EDWIN   Ah Tom! I thought you'd be out here. Couldn't see you in the melee, so I thought "sensible man's gone for a smoke out on the terrace". Brought some libation, old man.

TOM   Thank you, Sir Edwin. Decent of you. *(He takes the offered glass of scotch and raises it in a toast.)* To "Changing Times".

SIR EDWIN   Oh, "Changing Times" indeed!

     (They clink glasses and drink).

     I haven't had chance to ask you, old man – what on earth possessed you, at your age, to volunteer for this coming war? I shall be lost without you, you know. Can't find a lawyer as good as you. The estate, I fear, will go to pot without our weekly meetings!

TOM   Nonsense, Sir Edwin. You run this place like clockwork. We only have weekly meetings because you like to play cards afterwards!

SIR EDWIN   Mm. Well that's another thing! Where am I going to find someone as good at cribbage as you? Answer me that!

TOM   Archie Donaldson's a dab hand at crib...

SIR EDWIN   Donaldson! Can't abide the man! Every time I meet him he
               talks politics. Ever since he got elected on the Tory ticket
               he's been unbearable. Can't abide a politician who talks
               politics! Bad form and all that. Bad form. Anyway, you still
               haven't answered my question. Why, at the age of fifty one
               did you decide to volunteer?

TOM   *(embarrassed)* Oh, I don't know. I just didn't seem to have
               much purpose to my life, I suppose. Ever since Mary died...

SIR EDWIN   *(interrupting)* Ten years now, Tom. Hard to get over, I
               know – losing a young wife like that – but still, you should
               have got back in the saddle again, you should have
               remarried before now.

               *(They pause their conversation for a moment, as the
               orchestra finishes the waltz and there is a round of applause
               and general hubbub,)*

TOM   *(resuming)* There hasn't been anyone that I would have
               cared to marry and now I feel I'm beyond it. Got used to
               living alone. Anyway, surely the point of marriage is
               children? And I'm certainly past being interested in that!

SIR EDWIN   Good God, man! If I thought the purpose of marriage was
               children, I would never have done it! Can't stand either of
               my offspring– never could!

TOM   *(laughing)* You don't mean that, you old rogue! Why you
               were as proud as a peacock when your daughter married an
               Earl.

SIR EDWIN   Ah, you mistook relief for pride, old man. When Effie married into the nobility and managed to bag one of the few members of that class with actual money, I will admit that I broke open a few bottles of champagne – but that was pure relief that she was off my hands and I wouldn't have to support her anymore. For the last twenty five years her poor husband has had to pick up her dressmaker's bills; milliner's bills and God knows what other bills. Do you know that he said to me last year that Effie spends three thousand pounds a year on her wardrobe?!

TOM   Good God! That's more than your estate brings in a year!

(Another waltz strikes up inside the house but they do not pause in their conversation)

SIR EDWIN   I know, I know. I think she supports the whole of London's garment trade all by herself. I truly do. No, no-one in their right minds would marry to produce children! A civilised man marries a good woman in order that she may improve him – bring laughter, pleasant pursuits and delicacy into his miserable existence.

TOM   *(amused)* Is that what you truly believe?

SIR EDWIN   No sir! That's what my wife believes. Between you and me *(he looks around furtively and drops his voice to a loud whisper)* I think we all get married for a bit of legalised rumpy-pumpy, don't you?

TOM   *(laughing)* You're incorrigible!

(LADY MARJORIE enters at that point and overhears TOM. She is accompanied by VICTORIA.)

LADY M   *(smiling)* And what has he said that makes him so incorrigible?

TOM   Something far too rude for a lady's ears, I'm afraid!

LADY M	*(pretending to be scandalised)* Edwin! For shame!
SIR EDWIN	*(unrepentant)* Sorry m'dear but a man may say such things to another man that he may not say to a woman.
LADY M	Then I would venture that such things are not worth saying at all. Don't you agree, Victoria?
VICTORIA	I think, Lady Marjorie, that we must leave the men their little masculine chats, otherwise they might complain about our little feminine conversations.
SIR EDWIN	Ha! Well said, Miss Pelham! Well said!
LADY M	I'm so sorry, Tom – where are my manners?! Tom Pritchard, please let me introduce you to my very dear friend, Victoria Pelham.
TOM	*(taking VICTORIA's outstretched hand)* Very pleased to meet you.
VICTORIA	Likewise, Mr Pritchard.
LADY M	Now, Tom. Victoria does not care to dance and I know that you avoid it at all costs, so I am leaving her here for a spell, to be entertained by you, whilst I try to find my reprobate grandson, who has gone missing again with a whole decanter of sherry from the drawing room.
SIR EDWIN	What! That lad should have had a darn good thrashing when he was younger! *(turning to TOM)* What did I say to you about marriage and children? Well add grandchildren to my earlier sentiments! More trouble than they're worth!
LADY M	Come along, Edwin. *(She shepherds him towards the French windows)*. Two pairs of eyes are better than one. We need to find Jack before he consumes the whole decanter.

SIR EDWIN   I'm going to send his father a bill! That boy has seen off two bottles of my best claret in a week – and now the sherry...

(They exit. VICTORIA and TOM smile with amusement.)

TOM   He loves all his family dearly, you know, despite all the bluster.

VICTORIA   Sir Edwin? Yes, I gathered that he was just a cuddly bear really.

TOM   *(laughing)* Well, I've never heard him called that before! I shall never think of him in the same way again! Have you been friends with Lady Marjorie long?

VICTORIA   About two years. We serve together on two committees. One is a charity to help poor widows and the other – a new one just set up – is to help with the war effort.

TOM   Ah. And what will your war charity be doing, exactly? I'm sorry, won't you sit down first?

VICTORIA   Yes, thank you.

(They move towards one of the stone benches and sit side by side.)

Well, it's in its very early stages but just before I came here we had all agreed that it would be to provide comforts for the troops...

(TOM nearly chokes on his drink, as he is quite obviously thinking of a different "comfort" than is being meant.)

TOM   *(spluttering)* I'm sorry – did you say 'comforts'? Forgive me if I'm being inappropriate here but what sort of 'comforts' will a group of genteel ladies be providing for the troops?

VICTORIA	*(laughing)* Well not the saucy kind that you have in mind, obviously!
TOM	*(embarrassed)* I'm so sorry. I can't think what possessed me to say that!
VICTORIA	*(with mock outrage)* And me – a maiden lady of advancing years! Why sir! You forget yourself!
TOM	*(realising that she is a good sport and grinning sheepishly)* Yes, I was rather out of order, wasn't I? And anyway, you're not of advancing years…I mean… *(getting flummoxed)*…not yet…oh God! I've done it again! I'm sorry! I'm hopeless at this polite conversation lark!
VICTORIA	*(trying to suppress a smile)* Obviously. I suppose you're hopeless at dancing as well?
TOM	Absolutely.
VICTORIA	Confirmed bachelor or widower?
TOM	Widower.
VICTORIA	Oh, I'm sorry. Then you're excused everything.
TOM	I am?
VICTORIA	Absolutely. A confirmed bachelor has never learnt any graces. A widower has simply forgotten them.
TOM	Good. I must remember that. Are you hopeless at dancing?
VICTORIA	No. Actually I'm an excellent dancer. I'm just too old.
TOM	Pardon?
VICTORIA	I'm at that awkward age. I'm not young enough to be constantly asked to dance by all ages of men and I'm

	not old enough to be sat down and waited on hand and foot.
TOM	Forgive me but I would say that you were, however, just the right age for an intelligent conversation.
VICTORIA	*(beaming at him)* What a discerning man you are! But you'd better take advantage while you can.
TOM	Why? Are you going somewhere?
VICTORIA	No. But the window of opportunity is very small for intelligent conversation with women, didn't you know that?
TOM	How so?
VICTORIA	Well, according to my father, women have no sense when they are young, no time for conversation when they are raising a family and lose all their senses when they decline into old age. He has always maintained that you can only get a decent conversation out of a woman between the ages of forty and sixty.
TOM	He sounds like a rum cove, your father.
VICTORIA	Yes he is. And, I think, one of the few men I have ever respected.
TOM	Are you one of these Suffragettes, by any chance?
VICTORIA	No, I'm not. If a woman speaks her mind, does that automatically make her a radical?
TOM	No, not at all. But I suppose it might explain why someone as attractive as you has never been married.
VICTORIA	*(smiling)* How clever! Insult and flattery in the same sentence. I think I rather like you, Tom Pritchard.

TOM	*(smiling)* I think you may *grow* on me.
	(At that moment a giggling MAUD runs through the French windows and tries to hide behind a potted plant. She is pursued by a slightly drunk JACK, who is clutching a sherry decanter and two glasses. JACK is wearing the "Mess Dress" of a cavalry officer.)
JACK	You can't hide, Maud! I can see you! Now come along and take your medicine like a good little girl.
MAUD	*(giggling)* I shan't – you can't make me! I hate sherry anyway – and you're just trying to get me drunk!
JACK	Of course I am! *(swaying slightly and cornering MAUD)* How's a fellow supposed to get his wicked way with his fiancée unless he plies her with drink?
MAUD	Jack, you're so naughty!
TOM	*(to VICTORIA)* Excuse me. *(He goes up to JACK, who is trying to kiss a protesting but giggling MAUD).* Ah, there it is! Just what we need! *(He deftly takes the sherry decanter out of a surprised JACK's hand).* And glasses too! How did you know that we were dying for a sherry? *(He takes the glasses from JACK as well.)*
JACK	*(protesting)* I say!
TOM	*(pretending to be unconcerned)* I expect your grandmother told you to bring the sherry out to us. I must remember to thank her for her thoughtfulness before I leave tonight.
JACK	*(getting shirty)* Look here Pritchard....
TOM	*(firmly)* Captain Pritchard.
JACK	*(annoyed)* Your rank doesn't cut any ice with me,

	Pritchard. I'm a captain too – and in the Royal Hussars, which beats your infantry regiment at every turn.
TOM	Why does riding a horse make you superior, Jack?
JACK	*(sulkily)* It just does – everyone knows that.
TOM	And everyone knows that one should respect one elders. I may be a mere infantry captain but I outstrip you in age, boy. Never forget that.
JACK	(sullenly) Yes, sir.
TOM	Now run along, there's a good chap, and have a dance with your lovely young fiancée. It will help clear your head.
MAUD	*(tugging at JACK's arm)* Yes, come along, Jack. I'm dying for a dance. You know how much I love it.
JACK	*(glaring at TOM)* Yes, alright, I'm coming. *(muttering as he leaves)* Fellow can't have a bit of fun, without people interfering.
	(MAUD and JACK leave, arm in arm. TOM resumes his seat next to VICTORIA and offers her a glass.)
TOM	Sherry?
VICTORIA	Thank you.
	(TOM pours her a sherry and then pours himself one, placing the decanter under the bench afterwards.)
VICTORIA	I thought you handled that rather well.
TOM	What? Pouring sherry? It's one of my many talents.
VICTORIA	You know very well that I mean the situation with the oafish Jack.
TOM	Oh that. He's not such a bad fellow really. It's this war.

It's unsettled young chaps like him. They got caught up in the bravado of volunteering for King and Country and now they're all scared witless, I should imagine.

VICTORIA   Is that what happened to you?

TOM   How do you mean?

VICTORIA   Getting caught up in the bravado.

TOM   No. I had a pretty good idea that it wouldn't be all beer and skittles when I joined up.

VICTORIA   Then why did you do it? Was it because you felt you had to?

TOM   What? Didn't want to seem a coward and all that stuff?

VICTORIA   Yes.

TOM   No, not really. It's hard to explain. I had this conversation with Sir Edwin earlier. I don't know. Bored with my life, I suppose. Felt I should do my bit. Been living on my own too long, I think. Felt like I wanted to belong to something – some cause – some great endeavour. Does that make sense to you?

VICTORIA   Perfectly. That's what I've been doing all my life. What else does an intelligent woman do if marriage doesn't present itself and she has enough time and money to do as she pleases? That's why I do so much charity work. Why didn't you do something like that – instead of something as drastic as going to France to fight in a war that nobody really understands?

TOM   Oh I think everyone understands why we're in this war, don't they? I mean, we're doing the honourable thing by our allies and keeping the dreaded Boche from the gates of Britain. Isn't that what it's all about?

VICTORIA   *(reprovingly)* Now you're quoting propaganda at me.

TOM   Sorry. *(amused)* You know – you're a strange woman! All the other women I've met, since I've been in uniform, have gushed at me about how brave I am to be in the first wave of volunteers. Some have even kissed me, which was a bit startling!

VICTORIA   Well, I might very well be tempted to kiss you but it wouldn't be as a reward for going to war.

TOM   *(taken aback)* Good Lord! Is there no end to your boldness?

VICTORIA   *(laughing)* Have I shocked you? *(suddenly serious)* I think you may encounter far worse shocks in the days to come. I don't think this war is going to be over by Christmas, as they all keep saying, and I don't think it is going to be the jolly Gentleman's Duel that many men expect. Do you know that when the first battle of the American Civil War took place, ladies and gentlemen drove carriages out to a hill overlooking the battlefield – even took picnics! And when the fighting turned ugly and bloody, they all fled back home in distress. There must be nothing like watching a man being blown to bits by a cannon to put one off one's cucumber sandwiches.

TOM   Quite. I'll remember that when I'm under fire.

VICTORIA   I'm so sorry. It was thoughtless of me to be so blunt.

TOM   No, no. It's refreshing, somehow, to meet a woman who doesn't have a rose-tinted view of war.

(The orchestra strikes up "After the Ball is Over")

Good Lord! Is the ball ending already?

VICTORIA	Lady Marjorie said that, for the duration of the war, her entertainments would all be finished by ten, so that we can all get a good night's sleep.
TOM	Very sensible. Look – I am truly awful at dancing – but could you bear to dance this one with me? Out here on the terrace, of course. I can't cope with a crowded dance floor.
VICTORIA	*(smiling)* I'd be delighted.

(They stand up and take their positions in the centre of the terrace and begin a gentle waltz.)

TOM	Do you know, Miss Pelham, I've had an extraordinarily pleasant time talking to you tonight. I can't remember when I've had such interesting company.
VICTORIA	Thank you. Please call me Victoria. May I call you Tom, or do you prefer Thomas?
TOM	*(grimacing)* Lord no! Thomas is what my schoolmasters used to call me – usually before giving me a thrashing! Tom is what I prefer.
VICTORIA	A thrashing? I can't imagine you ever being naughty!
TOM	I wasn't really. I was usually in trouble for daydreaming. "Thomas Pritchard! You are gazing into space again. You are a dullard, boy!" was what they usually shouted at me.
VICTORIA	I was a daydreamer in school too.
TOM	Yes, I can imagine that. I should think your head has always been full of fascinating things.

*(TOM stops dancing for a moment and holds
VICTORIA at arm's length)*

Look here. I know it's very forward of me and we've
only just met but...can I write to you, when I'm in
France? I should like someone to write to. Would it be
alright?

VICTORIA   It would be just perfect. *(teasingly)* But I warn you – I'm
very demanding. I shall expect your best prose at least
once a month or I shall be very cross.

TOM   *(grinning)* Golly! What have I let myself in for?

VICTORIA   A jolly nice friendship, I hope, Tom Pritchard. Before
you leave, I'll give you my address in London. I shall be
working there all the time now, for the charities.

*(SIR EDWIN and LADY MARJORIE appear at the
French windows. The orchestra has finished and there is
a round of applause.)*

LADY M   I'm sorry I was away for so long, Victoria! I do hope
Tom has taken care of you?

VICTORIA   Tom has been perfect company, thank you.

LADY M   Come along, come along, both of you. We're about to
do the Toast.

*(LADY M ushers VICTORIA out. SIR EDWIN nudges
TOM.)*

SIR EDWIN   On familiar terms, I see. Calling you Tom. And getting
you to dance! My word, old man – you want to be
careful there! The companionship of a strong-minded
woman at your age could be too much for you, you
know!

TOM	*(smiling)* Oh, I don't know. I once heard that you can only get a decent conversation out of a woman when she's between the ages of forty and sixty.
SIR EDWIN	Really? Is that so? Well I'm blessed!
	(TOM and SIR EDWIN exit. The light is fading. From inside the house we hear LADY MARJORIE speaking.)
LADY M	*(offstage)* Ladies and gentlemen, I do hope you've all had a wonderful evening and that you will all raise your glasses to join my husband and I in the Loyal Toast.
SIR EDWIN	*(offstage)* Ladies and gentlemen, I give you "The King and our brave troops!. May they prevail over the enemy!"
MANY VOICES	*(offstage)* The King and our brave troops!
	(The lights go out and the sound of distant gunfire is heard. A spotlight comes up on one corner of the stage. TOM is sitting on the ground, wearing a helmet and writing a letter. His face is dirty.)
TOM	My dearest Victoria. Your letters finally arrived – the last three – and gave me great joy. Three month's worth of wonderful happiness, all in one day. It was almost too much for me to bear. You will have heard by now, in the newspapers at home, about the battle at Ypres in April. The Germans used poison gas against our front line and thousands of brave French colonial troops lost their lives. Thank God for the Canadians, who saved our bacon! They managed to push the Germans back but were then attacked themselves by the gas, against which we have no defence. We have been promised gas masks but they have not arrived yet. What a vile thing for the

Germans to use! My dear, it is a terrible thing to watch someone fighting for breath after being gassed. I had to take three of my men to the medical unit on the day of the first attack and I was horrified by what I witnessed. Thank God I have escaped that fate so far. I hear that we are now making gas to shoot over at the Germans. Much as we need to be able to retaliate, it makes me sad to think that we are descending to the level of the enemy. Such barbarity is surely monstrous between civilised countries! But what is the alternative? The Germans are routinely using gas at every attack now.

When your letters arrived, so did parcels of tobacco, soap and tinned rations. All the parcels had your charity's name on them and I was so proud. You are doing such wonderful work, my dear. Your little parcels truly do "comfort" the troops and I have to smile, remembering our first conversation about it all. I lose track of the time here now. Especially dates. But I always try and make the effort to remember August fifteenth – the day when we met. I was amused when your last letter described Lady Marjorie's recent ball. You are like a newspaper reporter when you describe the conversations of those at home. But I was sad that I could not be there with you – out on the terrace, in the warmth of an August evening.

I was also sad to hear of the loss of Sir Edwin's son-in-law. The Earl was Colonel of the regiment that is based just two miles along the line from us. By all accounts he was a very brave man and always chose to be in the thick of it, unlike most colonels, who choose to stay

back at HQ. I hope that Sir Edwin's grandson is still
alive. It would be too much for his daughter to bear if
she lost both husband and son in the same war.

I remembered, the other night, when I couldn't sleep,
young Jack saying that the Hussars were superior to
the infantry. Poor Jack! There is no such thing as cavalry
now! Horses would not survive old-fashioned cavalry
attacks but would be mown down by machine guns in
an instant. No, we are all foot soldiers now – unless
Jack has been fortunate enough to be deployed with his
horse doing behind the lines duty. All the horses are used
for moving heavy equipment and transporting supplies.

I think back to what I once called my "boring" life at
home. What I wouldn't give, Victoria my dear, for
some of that boredom now. The sound of shelling and
rifle fire is almost continuous – there is no peace.
Sometimes I think of when I used to wake up, alone, in
my bed at home – depressed by the solitude of it all – by
the silence, the lack of conversation after my wife died.
Now I would embrace total silence with open arms.
Except, of course, it wouldn't be total, if you were there.
How I long to talk to you again! A man might want for
nothing more than your company, I fancy.

Well, my dear, dear Victoria, I must close now, if I am to
catch the corporal who collects the post at four o'clock.
Strangely enough, my reliable old watch still works well
enough–despite the battering it has taken. It's just the
days of the week I can't remember. Nor the months or
seasons. All is just perpetual rain and an endless sea of
mud where I am.

I hope and pray that the sun is shining where you are.
I hope to see you at the next ball that Lady Marjorie holds.

Your loving friend,
Tom.

(The lights go dark and faint music from an orchestra
starts to play. The lights go up on the terrace again.
VICTORIA is sitting on one of the stone benches,
gazing out at the garden. She is reading a letter out loud.)

VICTORIA   I hope and pray that the sun is shining where you are. I
hope to see you at the next ball that Lady Marjorie holds.

Your loving friend,Tom.

(holding back the tears) Where are you Tom? I'm
waiting for you. Where are you?

(LADY M enters.)

LADY M   Oh, Victoria, there you are! Whatever are you doing,
sitting out here on your own?

VICTORIA   I wasn't in the mood to stay in the ballroom, Marjorie.
There are far too few men in there. It's depressing.

(LADY M sits next to her)

LADY M   Yes, dear, I know. I really shouldn't have held a ball this
year. It seems in bad taste. But the invitations were sent
out so long ago and I'm not privy to the battle plans of
the General Command.

VICTORIA   Eighty two thousand casualties in ten days and only one
hundred yards of the German lines taken. It doesn't bear
thinking about.

LADY M   What doesn't bear thinking about is that it is still raging! No-one can say for how long the battle of the Somme will continue. *(distraught and turning to VICTORIA)* Will we have any men left at the end of this war, my dear, will we?

(VICTORIA clasps LADY M's hand to comfort her. The music finishes and there is the faint sound of applause.)

VICTORIA   We've had two years of war now. Surely someone will come to their senses soon and put a stop to it all – before every nation in Europe wipes out the whole male population.

(MAUD rushes in crying.)

LADY M   *(rushing to comfort her)* Maud my dear! What is it? Tell me what's wrong?

MAUD   *(tearfully)* It's Jack. He's broken off our engagement.

LADY M   What! What an earth has got into that boy? Victoria, look after Maud, while I go and find Jack.

(VICTORIA goes and puts her arm around MAUD. Then JACK appears. In uniform. He has lost an arm and he has a patch over one eye. He looks scornful.)

Jack! What's this about breaking off your engagement?

JACK   Oh she's told you, has she?

LADY M   Well of course! You can see that the poor girl's devastated!

JACK   *(bitterly)* Is she. Has she told exactly what she's upset about?

LADY M   Of course! About you breaking off the engagement! I told you.

JACK   *(looking at MAUD intently)* But that's not the whole
              story, is it, Maud, my dear? You haven't quite told my
              grandmother the whole truth have you?

MAUD   *(evasively)* I don't know what you mean.

JACK   Oh I think you do.

LADY M   Jack, what is this nonsense?

JACK   Alright then. You may as well hear it, grandmother.
              I'm sure you can take it. You're a woman of the world.

LADY M   Jack. Behave yourself and stop tormenting people...

JACK   *(aggressively)* There was no point in continuing our
              engagement because Maud finds me repellent! She can't
              bear to look at me. Isn't that right Maud? Putting it
              bluntly, she doesn't want to go to bed with a man who
              has an arm and an eye missing.

LADY M   Jack! Apologise at once for speaking so crudely!

VICTORIA   No, no, Marjorie! I'm not offended. *(holding MAUD at
              arms length)* Is this true? What Jack says. *(shaking her
              slightly and being firm)* Is it true?

MAUD   *(wailing)* I can't help it if the sight of his...stump...makes
              me feel sick! I can't help it. And I won't touch it! My
              mother says you can catch gangrene from touching
              soldier's wounds!

LADY M   *(barely able to contain her anger)* Then your mother is a
              very stupid woman! What nonsense! *(her voice breaking
              as she turns to JACK)* Jack, I'm so sorry. You deserve
              better than this...this foolish girl...who needs to grow up,
              in my opinion!

VICTORIA   *(holding MAUD at arm's length and speaking very slowly and deliberately)* Do you know how many women would be grateful to get their man back and in their arms? Do you? Any man – in whatever condition – is better than no man at all! You stupid, stupid girl!

(VICTORIA breaks away from MAUD, runs to the bench, unable to stop crying. She cries softly but uncontrollably.)

LADY M   *(to JACK)* Now this has opened a whole can of worms and is far too important to be discussed here. My boy, you have had a raw deal all round and you and I must see that this is the last of it. Go and find your grandfather and have a stiff drink. I shall be with you shortly.

(JACK gives MAUD a last glare and exits.)

(to MAUD) As for you, my dear. I would be grateful if you would go and find your mother and ask her to take you home immediately. You are not welcome in my house anymore. I think we both know why.

MAUD   *(defiantly)* I knew it would all be my fault! I knew you would defend your precious Jack! Well what do you know? You have never had to make love to a…a… cripple and *(indicating VICTORIA)* she's just a dried up old spinster!

LADY M   *(beside herself)* Leave my house at once, you disgraceful girl!

(MAUD exits. LADY M rushes over to put her arms around VICTORIA.)

My dear, I'm so sorry! What a dreadful girl! I never
liked her much anyway but what a poisonous slut she
turned out to be!

VICTORIA   *(drying her eyes and smiling weakly)* But I wonder how
many more of them will be like Maud? Not the working
class women, of course. They'll have seen their men
maimed before – down the coalmines or in the factories.
They'll just get on with it and be glad of the fact that
they've got a man at all. No, it's the genteel middle class
women and the upper classes. How will they cope with
their men coming back minus a limb; or without sight
or worse – with no legs at all and in a wheelchair? You
and I have stood on the station platforms countless
times now and seen the wretched tide of wounded come
off the trains. Not even half a man, some of them.
We've dispensed tea and good cheer and tried not to cry
but – Marjorie...*(she starts to cry again)* it's so hard! It's
so hard to look them in the eyes and not flinch! It's so
hard not to show that sometimes we feel sick to our
stomachs at the sight of some of them! How can we
blame these young girls like Maud, who have never been
exposed to any of this horror, except when their
particular young man stands in front of them, mutilated
in some way? It must be so difficult for them to cope!
Life, for them, before the war, was all parties and
tennis and picnics – dashing young men who danced
with them and flirted with them. How can they be
expected to cope with the broken men that come back
from the front? How can they?

LADY M   You're right my dear, of course. I was too harsh on that girl. Lord knows, she wasn't the brightest button in the sewing box, in any event. I thought her pretty enough but she's never had any sense. Not the sort to be able to cope with Jack even when he was undamaged. She's right. It's not her fault. Boys like Jack – and even the older men – need some practical help once they've been wounded. They need support and the company of men in the same boat as themselves.

VICTORIA   *(laughing through her tears)* Do I sense another charity being born?

LADY M   *(chuckling)* Do you know, I think you do! It's just what's needed. A society for wounded ex-servicemen. I must speak to Archie Donaldson about it. Perhaps he can drum up some Government money! There! I feel better now! I always feel better when there's a project in hand!

VICTORIA   Perhaps you could involve Jack in it. Might do him some good.

LADY M   What a clever girl you are! He would be the perfect spokesman for such a charity! Young, still good-looking but terribly damaged in combat. I can see the cheque books being opened as we speak. What a clever girl you are!

VICTORIA   Not a girl, Marjorie. I haven't been a girl for a very long time.

LADY M   Nonsense! A woman is always a "girl" until she is a grandmother – and then she becomes an "old girl". Don't take any notice of Maud's jibe about being a spinster.

VICTORIA   She actually said 'a dried up old spinster' – if one were being accurate.

LADY M   Oh stuff and nonsense! It's not like you, Victoria, to be bothered by something that was said by a silly little girl. *(pausing and then her voice softens with concern)* Is there something else my dear? What is really upsetting you?

VICTORIA   *(starting to cry again)* Marjorie…do you think it is possible to be in love with someone you have only ever met once?

LADY M   *(understanding)* If you mean Tom Pritchard, I should think it perfectly possible. I've always been a little in love with him myself. Such a nice man and such good company.

VICTORIA   *(smiling through her tears)* I know. His letters, over the last two years have become so important to me and I feel as though I have known him forever…but now… I'm terribly afraid I've lost him…that I shall never see him again…and I can't bear it!

LADY M   My dear! What on earth has happened! Have you heard something?

VICTORIA   No. Nothing. That's just it. Tom has written to me every month for the last two years – except for the last three months, ever since this terrible battle started. I've heard nothing. But then, why would I? I'm not his wife, or sister or any other person who would be officially informed if he were wounded, missing in action or…dead.

LADY M   Well, he's not on any of the public lists of casualties. I

	know, because I religiously read them every week to see if any of the local women need some support.
VICTORIA	Dear Marjorie. Always thinking of the needs of others. What would we all do without you?
LADY M	Nonsense! Now look here, Victoria. There's been a bloody battle raging for the last three months. Probably running a postal service has been the last thing on the Army's mind. You'll see. Once this battle is over, you'll get a whole batch of Tom's letters at once. Mark my words.

(The orchestra strikes up "After the Ball is Over".)

Oh my goodness! The last waltz! I'm so sorry my dear... I must go and find Edwin. He'll want to do the loyal toast afterwards. Not that I feel much like toasting the King at the moment – or the Government! I never thought I'd say this, Victoria, but I think the whole lot of them are just a pack of warmongers – I really do! *(She plants a kiss on VICTORIA's cheek.)* Now will you be alright my dear?

VICTORIA	Yes, yes. I'll be fine. You go and find Edwin.
LADY M	*(making for the French windows)* I shall be back as soon as I can.
VICTORIA	Don't worry. *(realising that LADY M has gone, she starts talking to herself)* No, I won't be fine. Inside I'm breaking apart. I can't bear the waiting.

(While she is speaking, we see LADY M leading a limping figure into view. He has his head bandaged, one hand bandaged and, with the other hand he is gripping a walking stick, which he is using because one leg is

completely stiff. It is TOM. LADY M has a
handkerchief to her eyes. She points towards
VICTORIA, gives TOM a big hug and leaves him alone.
TOM limps awkwardly on to the terrace and stands
there listening to VICTORIA)

I wish I could say to Tom that he has conquered me.
This heart, which I thought was made of ice...that no
man would ever impress me enough to thaw it out...has
melted under his onslaught of thoughtful and loving
letters. But I'm terribly, terribly afraid, that having
waited so long for the right man – I have now lost my
chance. That I will never see him again – and that will
be like a long slow death for me...

TOM   *(softly)* You do know that talking to yourself is the first
sign of madness, don't you?

(VICTORIA, at the sound of his voice, does not turn
round but she clasps her hand to her mouth to stop
herself from crying. She is almost unable to believe what
she hears.)

VICTORIA   *(struggling to compose herself)* Is hearing voices the
second sign of madness? – Tom, are you really there?

TOM   I'm here, my dearest. What's left of me...

(VICTORIA turns and then rushes to TOM and takes
him fiercely in her arms. He buries his head in her neck
for a moment and puts his bandaged hand around her
waist.)

TOM   *(raising his head)* Steady on, old girl. I might topple over!

VICTORIA   *(releasing him and springing back in alarm)* Oh my God,

	Tom, have I hurt you? I didn't think......
TOM	*(smiling and pulling her back towards him)* I was joking. I could happily stay in your arms forever.
VICTORIA	Is that a proposal?
TOM	Possibly. *(seriously)* If you fancy spending most of your time nursing a man with a gammy leg and half a ton of shrapnel about his person. Not something to be taken on lightly.
	(slight tinge of bitterness) Of course, I forgot to mention the nightmares and the shell shock. A man who shakes uncontrollably when he hears a sudden loud noise is pretty unattractive to a woman, I would imagine.
VICTORIA	*(Laying a finger on his lips to silence him and speaking firmly)* Be quiet. I would have thought, after eavesdropping on me just now – which, by the way, was most ungentlemanly – *(TOM grins)* you would have realised that I would take you whatever state you are in. If they had brought you home in a basket, I would have taken you. So long as you can speak to me and hear me. As long as we can nourish each other's souls – I am content. I don't care if we only have a few years together – it will be enough. As long as you love me. You do love me, don't you?
TOM	With all my heart.
VICTORIA	And do your injuries mean that you don't have to go back to war?
TOM	They do. I have been honourably discharged. No more army for me.

(Music stops. Applause. LADY M and a beaming SIR EDWIN appear in the French windows. LADY M restrains SIR EDWIN from interrupting the two lovers.)

VICTORIA   Then I see no reason why we can't get married straight away.

TOM   *(smiling)* I'll leave you to organise it then. I'm pleading uselessness on all fronts.

LADY M   *(unable to restrain herself any longer)* She'll do more than that! She'll let *me* organise the wedding!

SIR EDWIN   *(rushing forward and trying to shake TOM's hand but having to settle for shaking his raised walking stick)* Pritchard, you old devil! Thank God you're back! Playing cribbage with Archie Donaldson has been more than body and soul can bear!

LADY M   *(reprovingly)* Edwin!

TOM   *(Looking at his bandaged hand)* Well, I'm not quite up to playing cards yet, old man, but I have to warn you that two years of waiting around in the trenches have turned me into a pretty fiendish card player.

SIR EDWIN   *(delighted)* I shall look forward to it!

LADY M   Edwin, it's time to do the loyal toast. Come along.

SIR EDWIN   Oh bugger the loyal toast!

LADY M   *(shocked)* Edwin! This war has certainly made your language riper, that's for sure!

SIR EDWIN   Sorry, m'dear. I suppose I'd better go and do it. Talk to you later, Pritchard. Wonderful news all round eh?

(LADY M and SIR EDWIN exit. The orchestra finishes.

Applause. TOM and VICTORIA go and sit on the
stone bench. TOM's damaged leg doesn't bend, so it
sticks out awkwardly. VICTORIA puts her arm
through his and leans her head gently on his
shoulder. They gaze out over the garden.)

SIR EDWIN   *(offstage)* Ladies and gentlemen, I propose to depart
from the usual Loyal Toast this time. I'm sorry if
that seems shocking to some of you but – well –
times have changed, as we all know. So, ladies and
gentlemen, please raise your glasses in a toast to
those who have returned to us and those who will
never return. Ladies and gentlemen, I give you
"Friends Lost and Friends Returned."

VOICES
OFFSTAGE
and VICTORIA
and TOM   *(They smile at each other as they say...)* Friends Lost
and Friends Returned.

BLACKOUT.

Music swells   *("After the Ball is Over")*

THE END.

FURNITURE LIST

Two "stone benches" and two ornamental plants in large stone pots. *(See set plan)* Low ornamental walls could be added.

PROPERTY LIST

LIGHTING AND EFFECTS PLOT

See page opposite the Cast List.

To open: LIGHTS: *general lighting denoting a summer's evening, exterior.*

SFX: *Faint music from small orchestra (waltz)playing inside the house.*

Page 2:   cue: SIR EDWIN: "...you should have married before now."

SFX: *Orchestra finishes, followed by applause.*

Page 3:   cue: TOM: "That's more than your estate brings in a year!"

SFX: *Orchestra strikes up again.*

Page 3 – 7:   *At any time during these pages, the music playing can draw to a close, to be followed by applause.*

Page 11:   cue: TOM: "...to meet a woman who doesn't have a rose-tinted view of war."

SFX: *Orchestra strikes up "After the Ball is Over."*

Page 13:   cue: VICTORIA: "I shall be working there all the time now, for the charities."

SFX: *Music finishes, followed by applause.*

Page 14:   cue: SIR EDWIN: "May they prevail over our enemy!"

SFX: *Lots of voices : "The King and our brave troops!"*

LIGHTS: *Fade to black. Spotlight comes up on TOM on front corner of the stage.*

SFX: *Distant sound of shelling, which continues until next cue on page 17.*

Page 17:   cue: TOM: "Your loving friend, Tom."

              LIGHTS: *Fade spotlight to black. Raise lights slowly on main set.*

              SFX: *Fade in orchestra music before and during lights going up on main set.*

Page 18:   cue: LADY M: "Will we have any men left at the end of the war, my dear, will we?"

              SFX: *Music finishes, followed by applause.*

Page 24:   cue: LADY M: "...you'll get a whole batch of Tom's letters at once. Mark my words."

              SFX: *Orchestra strikes up "After the Ball is Over."*

Page 26:   cue: TOM: "I have been honourably discharged. No more army for me."

              SFX: *Music stops followed by applause.*

Page 28:   cue: SIR EDWIN: "Ladies and gentlemen, I give you,

              "Friends Lost and Friends returned."

              SFX: *many voices offstage: "Friends Lost and Friends Returned."*

              LIGHTS : *Fade to black.*

              SFX: *Fade up "After the Ball is Over."*

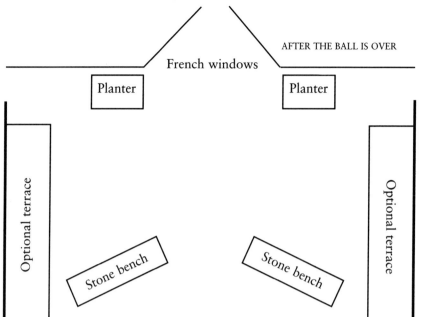

French windows

Planter

Planter

Optional terrace

Optional terrace

Stone bench

Stone bench

Aerial view

Note: Allow room in front for TOM's dugout.

SET PLAN

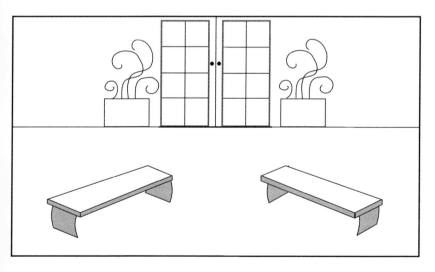

Audience view